W9-ADL-616

The Jimi Hendrix Experience

Edited by
MARCUS HEARN

Designed by
JAMES KING

TITAN BOOKS

The Jimi Hendrix Experience
ISBN: 9780857685551

Titan Books
A division of Titan Publishing Group Ltd.
144 Southwark St.
London
SE1 0UP

This edition: October 2011
10 9 8 7 6 5 4 3 2 1

First published in the UK 2005.

Front cover: Herb Schmitz
Frontispiece: Marc Sharratt
Title page: Dezo Hoffman

Designed by James King.

Did you enjoy this book? We love to hear from our readers. Please e-mail us at: readerfeedback@titanemail.com or write to Reader Feedback at the above address.

To receive advance information, news, competitions, and exclusive offers online, please sign up for the Titan newsletter on our website: **www.titanbooks.com**

A CIP catalogue record for this title is available from the British Library.

Printed and bound in China.

From left to right: Mitch Mitchell, Jimi Hendrix and Noel Redding
– The Jimi Hendrix Experience. Photograph: Bruce Fleming

INTRODUCTION

'You have a lot of groovy groups here in England but some of the sounds are just too clean. You can't expect deep feeling to come out of music put down on bits of paper with arrangements. I feel everything I play – it's got to be inside you.' **Jimi Hendrix, 1967**

James Marshall Hendrix was born in Seattle, Washington, on Friday 27 November 1942.

After getting out of the Army he embarked on a busy, but unfulfilling, career as a guitarist for such artists as the Isley Brothers, Sam Cooke and Little Richard.

In September 1966 he was playing at a club in New York's Greenwich Village when he was spotted by Bryan 'Chas' Chandler, the former bassist with Newcastle beat group the Animals. Chandler was so impressed by what he saw that he decided to bring Hendrix to England and, together with Animals manager Michael Jeffery, launch his career. Hendrix and Chandler left New York on Saturday 24 September 1966.

Hendrix never grew accustomed to English food, but he enjoyed almost every other aspect of London life. He met his girlfriend, Kathy Etchingham, on the day he arrived (the black rose-patterned shirt he wears in some of the shots in this book was a present from her). Less than a week later he mustered sufficient chutzpah to join Cream onstage. Within minutes his dazzling guitar skills

had reduced an envious Eric Clapton to a state of despair.

Hendrix was in favour of leading a larger group of backing musicians, but Chandler persuaded him to form a power trio in the style of Cream. Following a brief round of auditions Hendrix and Chandler selected Noel Redding to play bass. Redding had previously tried out for the Animals and had spent some time in an unsuccessful group called the Loving Kind. A rhythm guitarist by inclination, the switch to bass took some adjustment. Days later, Hendrix and Redding were joined by John 'Mitch' Mitchell, a former child actor and accomplished jazz drummer who had recently completed a year with Georgie Fame's Blue Flames.

By the second week in October 1966 the three-piece had a stable line-up, and a name – the Jimi Hendrix Experience. The origins of the name are difficult to pinpoint – Redding claimed it was Jeffery's idea, while Mitchell says Chandler thought of it in New York, shortly after meeting Jimi. Whatever the inspiration, it was an apt description of a group of young musicians who had to be heard to be believed. They played their first concerts, supporting French rocker Johnny Halliday, in mid-October. By the end of the month they had returned to London and started work on their first single.

'Hey Joe' was released in December 1966. In January

Photograph: Harry Goodwin

Keith Altham alerted readers of the *New Musical Express* to Hendrix by describing him as a 'one-man guitar explosion, with a stage act that leaves those who think pop has gone pretty with their mouths hanging open. What this man does to a guitar could get him arrested for assault.'

The flashpoint year for the Jimi Hendrix Experience was 1967. 'Hey Joe' was followed into the charts by 'Purple Haze', arguably the group's quintessential single. The first album, *Are You Experienced*, was released in May. As well as featuring such outstanding tracks as 'Foxy Lady', 'Manic Depression' and 'Fire', *Are You Experienced* pushed the boundaries of studio experimentation and was a milestone in that year's cultural shift from pop to rock, and singles to albums. It remains quite probably the greatest debut in rock history.

Hendrix returned to America in a (literal) blaze of glory when the Experience played the Monterey Festival in June 1967. Back in England, the group built on their success with their second album, *Axis: Bold As Love*, which was released at the end of the year. This was a more mature collection of songs that continued to illustrate the group's impressive versatility, from the thunderous 'Spanish Castle Magic' to the trippy

'If 6 Was 9' and the fragile 'Little Wing'.

The Experience reached the pinnacle of their studio achievements with their third, and final, album. The *Electric Ladyland* double LP was released in 1968 and cast the group in an epic soundscape that enveloped such diverse songs as 'Crosstown Traffic', 'Burning of the Midnight Lamp' and a definitive cover of Bob Dylan's 'All Along the Watchtower'. Side four closed with 'Voodoo Child (Slight Return)', its portentous lyrics and shimmering guitars suggesting that even better was yet to come.

By the time *Electric Ladyland* was released, however, Hendrix was starting to lose his way. He had already parted company with producer Chas Chandler, and in 1969 the Experience split up. Hendrix continued to record and perform, but he never completed another studio album.

Jimi Hendrix returned to London in September 1970, aiming to reunite with Chas Chandler in an effort to regain some focus to his career. On 18 September Hendrix died in his sleep, his death the result of accidental barbiturate intoxication. His future was one of tantalising promise. His legacy is one of inestimable value.

The Jimi Hendrix Experience were celebrities in the London scene of the mid- to late-1960s, so it's not surprising that the photographers of Rex Features seemed to follow them almost everywhere they went. This book's emphasis is therefore on the period when the Experience established their reputation and capitalised on their early success.

Most of the pictures in this book hail from January to December 1967, and illustrate what it must have been like to have been in the eye of that psychedelic storm: David Magnus photographs Hendrix on the doorstep of his new West London home, the young musician clearly proud of his new status. Herb Schmitz captures Hendrix and his friends (including Eric Clapton) in the relaxed haven of a subterranean London club,

while Bruce Fleming's pictures show the group's progress from awkward teen pin-ups to confident studio musicians. And the Hungarian photographer Dezo Hoffman shows why he was a favourite of magazine editors and stars alike, with a session that starts with Hendrix dressed as Santa and finishes with him posing for the magnificent shots that would adorn his biggest-selling album.

Thanks, as ever, to the librarians and other staff at Rex Features, and to New Business Manager Glen Marks for his advice and encouragement. Thanks also to Andrew Godfrey and Reg Page for additional scanning and image restoration.

It *has* been a long time, as Hendrix once said, but many of these pictures are timeless.

Pages 8-13 ✂
Early group shots and portraits, the first of which was at one point considered for use on the cover of the band's first album, *Are You Experienced*.

The military dress jacket worn by Hendrix became something of a trademark and was typical of the vintage gear found in I Was Lord Kitchener's Valet and other such London boutiques.

Soon after arriving in England Hendrix was stopped by a policeman and told to take the jacket off, on the grounds that it was disrespectful to the soldiers who had died wearing such uniforms. Hendrix was possibly recalling this incident when, in January 1967, he told the *New Musical Express* that he wore the jacket out of respect. 'Maybe the guy who wore this coat got killed in action,' he said. 'Would people rather his coat be hung up and go mouldy somewhere to be forgotten like him? Men like that should not be forgotten and if I wear this coat I remember. Anyway, I wear it because it's comfortable!'

Photographs: Bruce Fleming (pages 8-9), Harry Goodwin (pages 10-13)

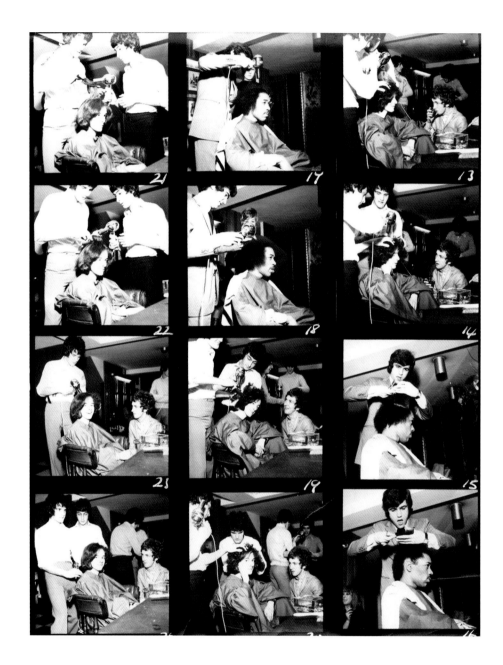

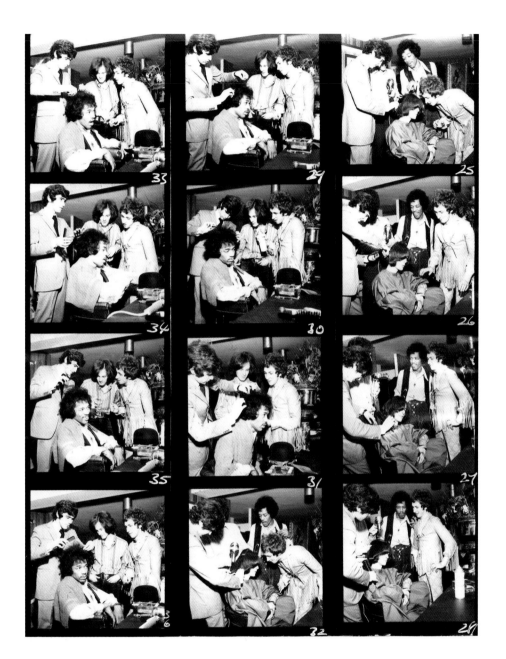

Pages 14-19

Hendrix was very particular about his hair. One of the few possessions he brought from America was a set of rollers.

'I wear my hair long because that's the way I like it,' he said in January 1967. 'It was long in New York and it's longer now because young people here are more open-minded in their attitudes.'

Photographs: Bruce Fleming

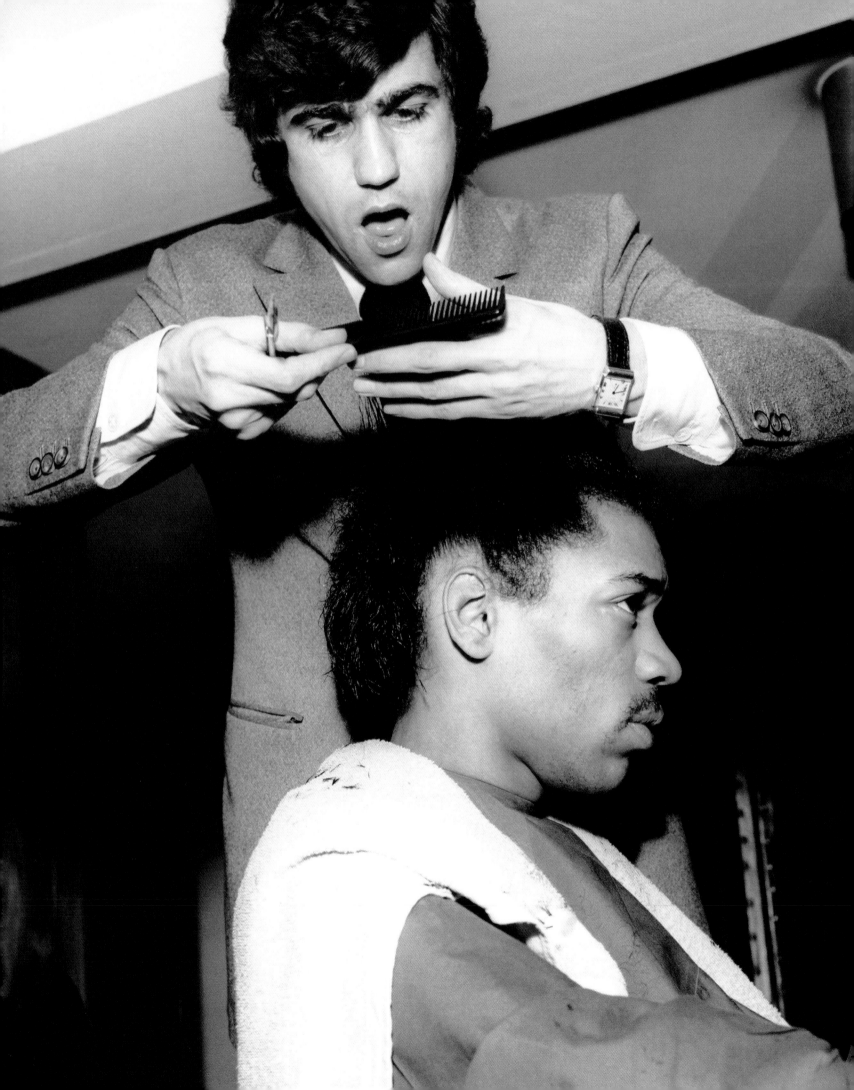

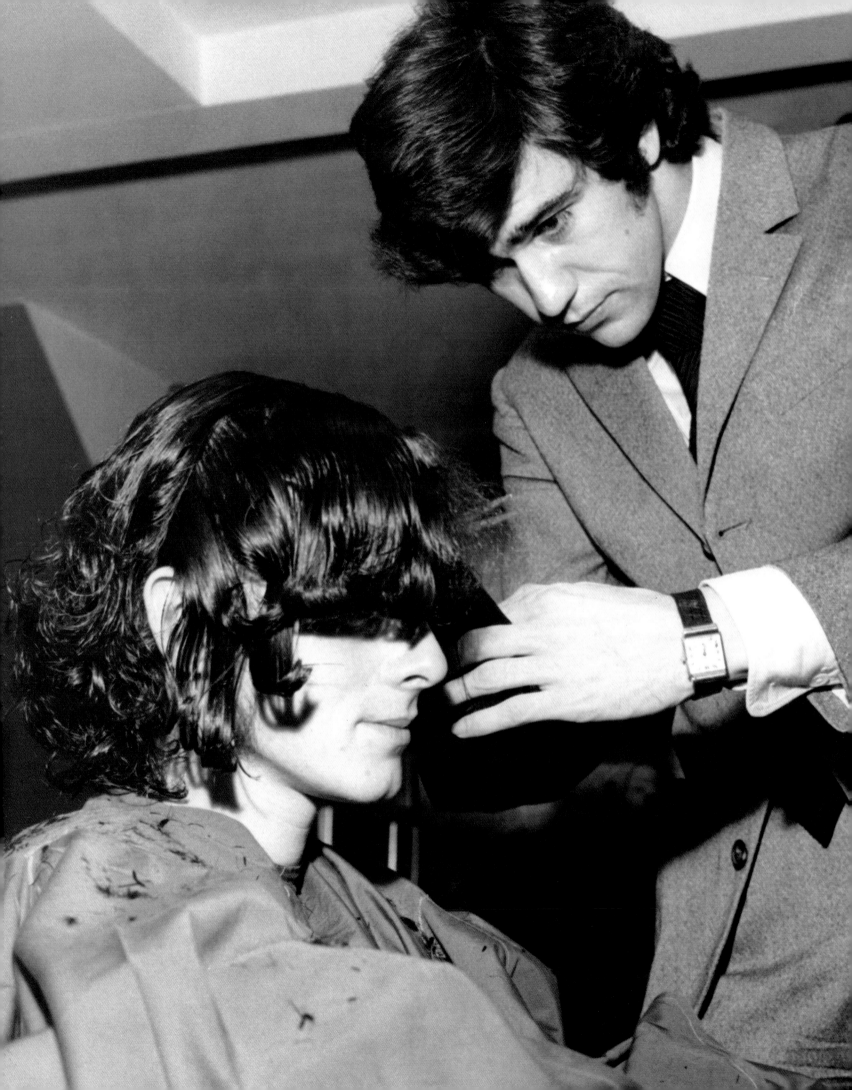

Pages 20-41

After months of living hand to mouth, Hendrix and his girlfriend Kathy Etchingham moved into the ground floor of 34 Montagu Square, London, at the end of 1966. The flat's owner, Ringo Starr, had loaned it to Chas Chandler as a favour.

This iconic photo session dates from February 1967 and shows Hendrix posing on the pavement nearby. He is wearing a badge bearing the name of his hero, Bob Dylan, and at one point mocks his own short-sightedness by posing with a pair of old-fashioned spectacles.

Later in 1967 Hendrix was obliged to leave Montagu Square because, Chandler claimed, unhappy neighbours invoked a clause forbidding black tenants.

Photographs: David Magnus

CITY OF WESTMINSTER
MAXIMUM 2 HOURS
6d FOR EACH HOUR
Monday - Friday

Pages 44-45 ✂

On Tuesday 9 May 1967 Hendrix attended a 'Tribute to the Recording Industry' event at the Dorchester Hotel. As this was a formal luncheon hosted by the Variety Club, he was on his best behaviour.

Photographs: Dezo Hoffman

Pages 46-51 ✂

Against their better judgement, the Jimi Hendrix Experience joined some unlikely co-stars for a month-long package tour in spring 1967. The group was third-billed behind Cat Stevens and headliners the Walker Brothers. Easy listening crooner Engelbert Humperdinck was 'special guest'. These pictures were taken backstage at the Astoria in Finsbury Park, London, on Friday 31 March, the second day of the tour.

At the suggestion of journalist Keith Altham, Hendrix decided to relieve the tedium with a new example of his legendary showmanship. During that night's performance of 'Fire', Hendrix astonished the audience by doing something he'd never done before – he laid his guitar on the stage, smothered it in lighter fuel and set light to it. Mitch Mitchell remembers it well: 'All these irate people and fire chiefs appeared and of course we were told, "You'll never work in this theatre again." And do you know I don't think we ever did.'

The pictures on pages 48 and 50 show (left to right): Hendrix, Cat Stevens, the Walker Brothers' Gary Leeds and Engelbert Humperdinck.

Photographs: Barry Peake

Pages 52-59

Hendrix first met Eric Clapton, arguably Britain's greatest rock and blues guitarist, at a Cream gig at the London Polytechnic on Saturday 1 October 1966. 'Jimi came on and stole the show,' recalls Clapton. 'He did his whole repertoire. He did a fast Howlin' Wolf song. Very powerful. He played the guitar behind his head, between his legs, with his teeth, slapped it round on the ground a bit. I just went, "Yeah – this is it! This guy is bound for glory."'

Chas Chandler later found Clapton with his head in his hands. Clapton looked up and said, 'You didn't tell me he was *that* fucking good!'

Clapton and Hendrix became friends, as evidenced in the shots from pages 54 to 56, but a simmering rivalry remained.

Photographs: Herb Schmitz

Pages 60-63 ✂

Thursday 2 March 1967: a brief performance at the Marquee Club for the German television programme *Beat Club aus London*. The group always preferred playing live for TV shows, and Hendrix in particular was uncomfortable about miming. 'It's so phoney,' he said in January that year. 'If you want to scream and holler at a record you can do that at home – I'm strictly a live performer.'

Photographs: Marc Sharratt (page 60), Ray Stevenson (pages 62-63)

Pages 64-69

An encounter with the Who, a group Hendrix came to admire and respect during his stay in England. 'It was a shock to see somebody like Hendrix,' says Pete Townshend. 'We were witnessing something really quite remarkable.'

The Who's co-manager, Kit Lambert, was similarly impressed, signing the Jimi Hendrix Experience to his independent label Track Records.

Townshend's guitar-smashing had earned him a reputation as one of rock's most flamboyant showmen, but he was aware he had met his match with Hendrix. When the Who and the Jimi Hendrix Experience were both scheduled to play the closing night of the Monterey International Pop Festival Townshend flatly refused to let his group follow Hendrix for fear of being upstaged.

Photographs: Barry Peake

Page 71-75

Booked at the recommendation of Paul McCartney, the Jimi Hendrix Experience made their US debut at Monterey on Sunday 18 June 1967.

As Hendrix and Redding tuned up, the Rolling Stones' Brian Jones introduced the relatively unknown group to the crowd of 20,000. The Experience hit the ground running with a blistering version of Chester Burnett's 'Killing Floor'. Other highlights of an outstanding show included a seismic 'Foxy Lady' and their British hit 'Purple Haze'.

The Experience ended their set with a sledgehammer cover of the Troggs' 'Wild Thing'. At the end of the song Hendrix produced a can of lighter fuel and set light to his guitar. Stoned audience-members gazed wide-eyed as Hendrix fanned the flames on stage before smashing the burning guitar into pieces.

After the gig Mike Jeffery berated the group for having damaged a microphone stand, but that was surely a small price to pay.

The Jimi Hendrix Experience had arrived.

Photographs: Bruce Fleming

Pages 76-91

'Jimi wasn't tall, but when posed with us flanking him he photographed larger than life,' recalled Noel Redding. 'The three of us looked really good together – symmetrical.'

This light-hearted London session was briefly interrupted by a traffic warden asking for Jimi's autograph. A reversed version of the group shot on page 88 now appears on the cover of the 1998 compilation *BBC Sessions*.

Photographs: Joel Elkins

Pages 92-107

Producer Chas Chandler supervises the recording of *Axis: Bold As Love* at Olympic Studios in October 1967.

Eddie Kramer, who was the principal sound engineer on these sessions, believes that Chandler brought a disciplined sensibility to Hendrix's music. 'I think Jimi was forced into condensing this amazing talent into highly polished little pieces,' he says. 'Chas was largely instrumental in shaping that talent and bringing it to the fore and helping Jimi express himself.'

Axis would prove to be Noel Redding's favourite Experience album: 'We felt positive and reasonably relaxed during the sessions, trying to take our own time, even though it was made plain that at least three record companies were drumming their fingers, anxiously awaiting the product.'

Photographs: Bruce Fleming

Pages 108-137

On Thursday 7 December 1967 the Jimi Hendrix Experience took part in a lengthy photo session which would result in some of the best-known images of the band.

Things got off to an unorthodox start when Hendrix was persuaded to pose as Santa Claus presenting the ideal Christmas gift – a copy of *Axis: Bold As Love*, which had been released the previous Friday. The shot above featured on the front of *Record Mirror* less than two weeks later.

This session also resulted in the pictures that would form the composite used on the sleeve of *Smash Hits* in 1968. This compilation would prove to be the most successful of all the Experience albums released during Hendrix's lifetime. Two of the photographer's experimental composites are presented on pages 136 and 137.

Photographs: Dezo Hoffman

117

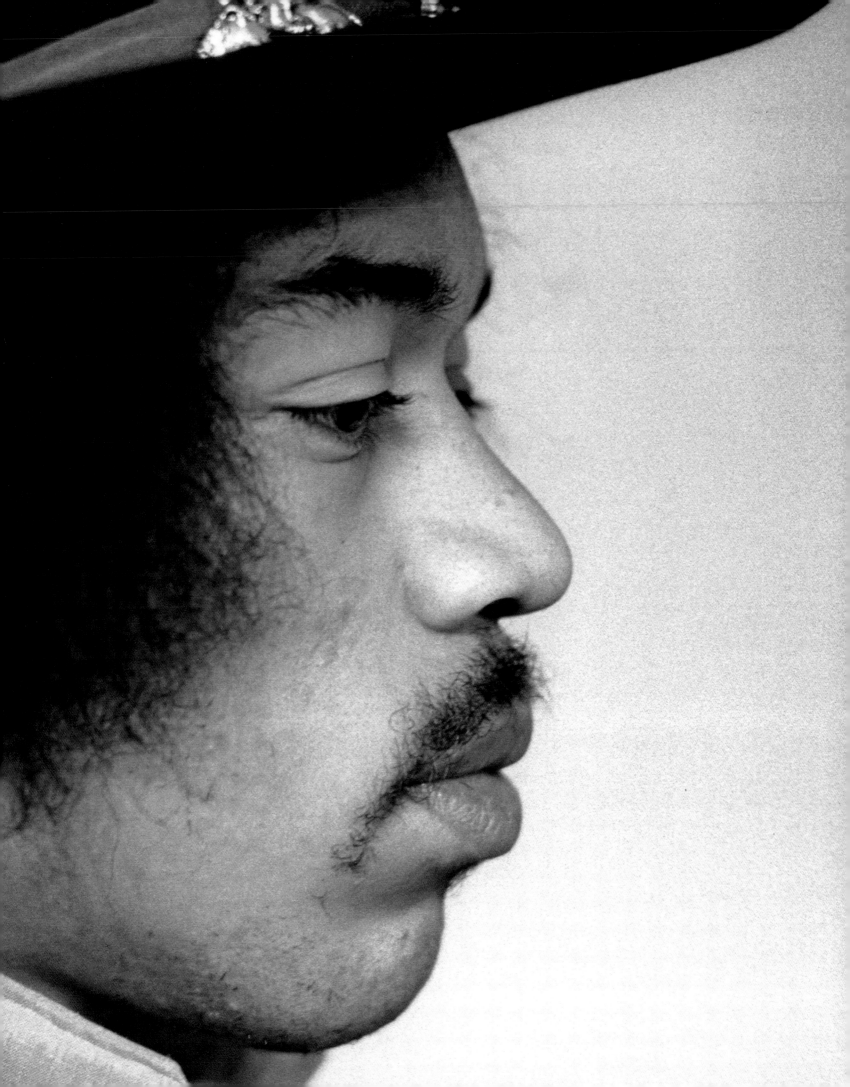

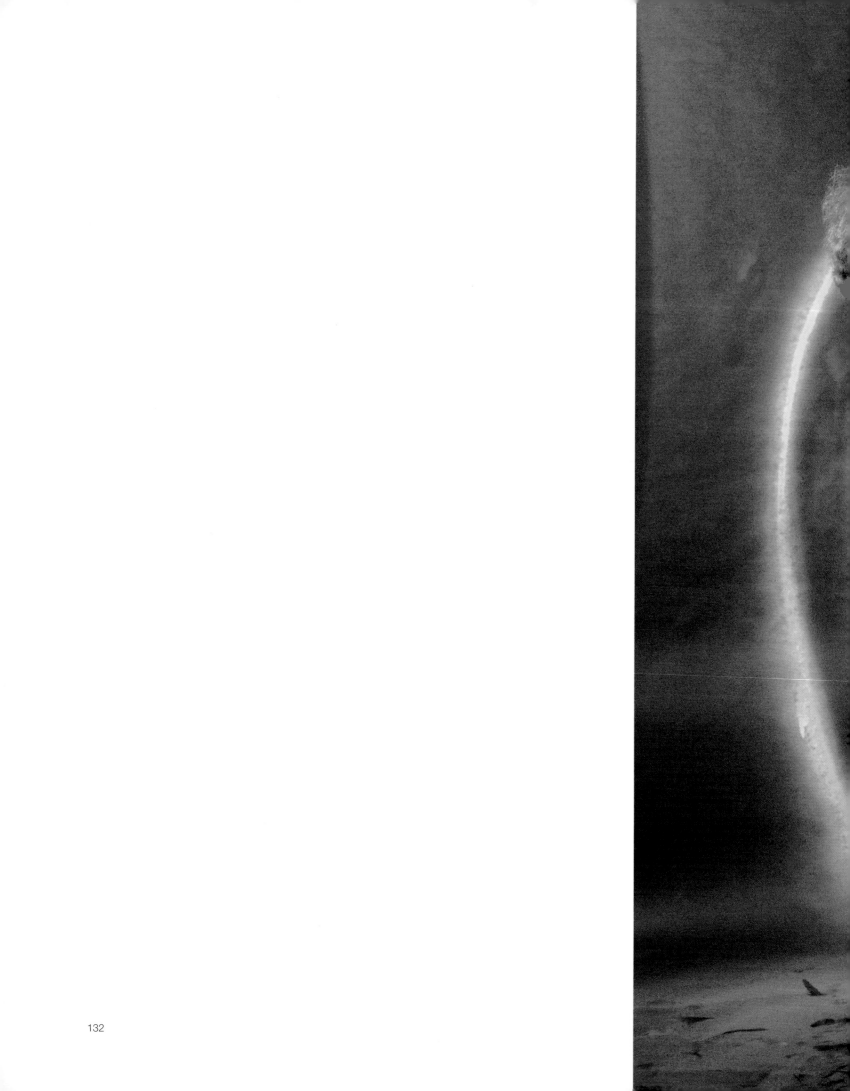

Pages 138-147
Friday 15 December 1967: Hendrix plays his white Stratocaster with his teeth during the recording of a session for *Top Gear* at the Playhouse Theatre in Charing Cross, London. The session, which was broadcast by Radio One on Christmas Eve, comprised superb new versions of 'Wait Until Tomorrow', 'Spanish Castle Magic', 'Hear My Train A Comin'' and an energetic cover of the Beatles' 'Day Tripper'. The band even found time to record an impromptu jingle for the radio station.

Photographs: R. Miles

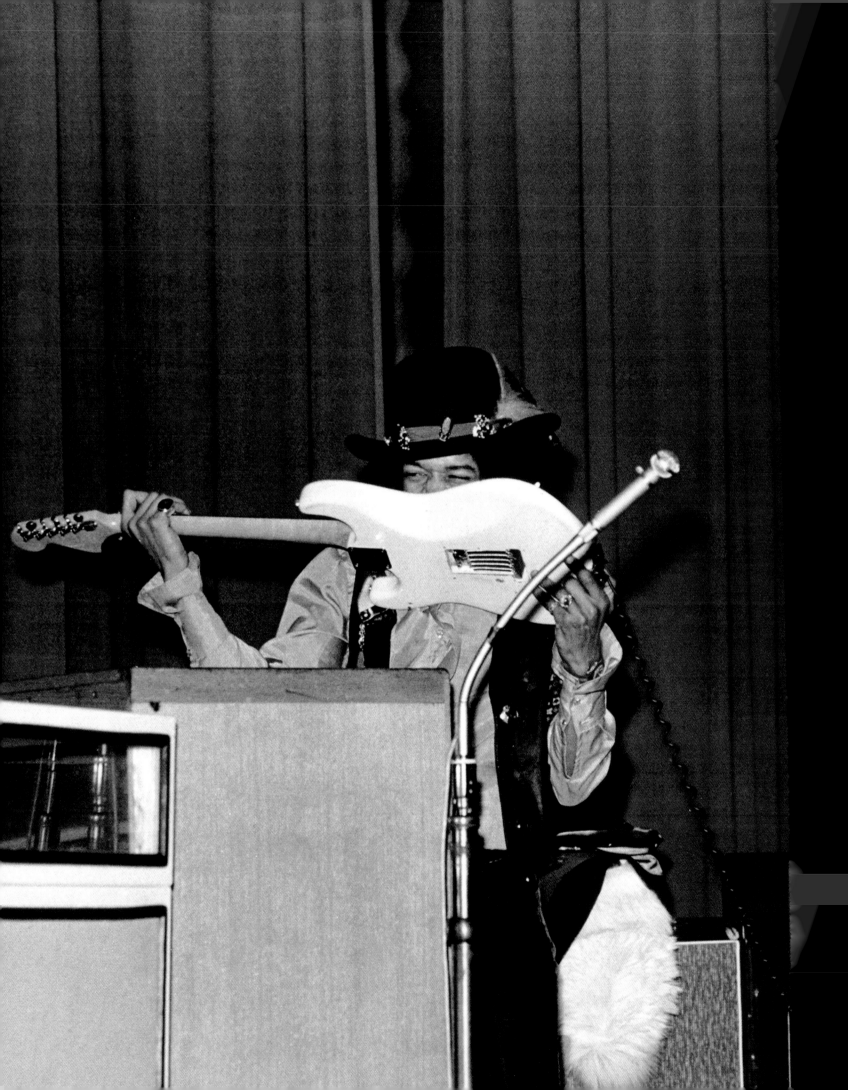

Pages 149-153

By 1968 musical and business frustrations had caused the Jimi Hendrix Experience to unravel. Following a series of lacklustre performances on European and US tours in the first half of 1969, the group disbanded. Hendrix would ultimately retain Mitch Mitchell as his drummer, but Noel Redding was never invited to return. 'It's hard to imagine three people with less in common,' said Redding, 'a country boy, a theatre school suburbanite, and a city kid. It made for good music but we were spending more time together than a married couple.'

Photographs: Bill Zygmant

Pages 154-157

The Royal Albert Hall, Saturday 18 February 1969. A troubled Hendrix poses for photographers during a sound check for that evening's performance. The show is the first of two at the Albert Hall, the latter of which will prove to be the Experience's final British concert.

Although by this time Hendrix had parted company with Chas Chandler he turned to his old friend for help. 'When I arrived for rehearsals and sound checks Hendrix was having trouble with feedback through his amplifiers and there was also interference in the recording equipment,' Chandler told John McDermott. 'It was a shambles. I ended up running the shows for him, trying to get everything right. I hadn't been hired; I was there to help out friends.'

This concert, along with the 24 February show in the same venue, was filmed by Steve Gold and Jerry Goldstein. A dispute over rights has prevented their film from ever being released.

Photographs: André Csillag

Pages 158-159

It was cold and inhospitable when Jimi Hendrix stepped onto the stage at the Isle of Wight Festival in the early hours of Monday 31 August 1970. He had been reluctant to leave his recently completed studio, Electric Lady, and had flown straight from the opening party in New York. 'It *has* been a long time, hasn't it?' a weary Hendrix told the audience as he launched into his first UK concert since the Albert Hall shows of February 1969.

'It was just a lousy performance,' says Mitch Mitchell, although he, Hendrix and bassist Billy Cox eventually warmed up enough to play a memorable two-hour set.

It would prove to be Hendrix's farewell to the country that made him a star. Eighteen days later he was dead.

Photographs: Brian Moody

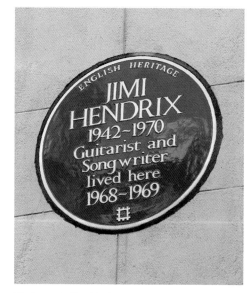

Photograph: Ilpo Musto

REFERENCES

Articles

Altham, Keith. 'Wild Jimi Hendrix'. *New Musical Express*, 14 January 1967

Anon. 'Pop Think In'. *Melody Maker*, 28 January 1967

Anon. '*Are You Experienced* review'. *Melody Maker*, 28 May 1967

Anon. 'Jimi Hendrix obituary'. *The Times*, 19 September 1970

Jones, Nick. '*Axis: Bold As Love* review'. *Melody Maker*, 9 December 1967

King, John. 'Scene's Wildest Raver!'. *New Musical Express*, 28 January 1967

Books

Etchingham, Kathy with Andrew Crofts. *Through Gypsy Eyes*. London: Victor Gollancz, 1998

Glebbeek, Caesar and Douglas J. Noble. *Jimi Hendrix: The Man, The Music, The Memorabilia*.
   Limpsfield and London: Paper Tiger, 1996

Marsh, Dave. *Before I Get Old*. London: Plexus, 1983

McDermott, John with Eddie Kramer. *Hendrix: Setting the Record Straight*. London: Little Brown, 1992

McDermott, John with Billy Cox and Eddie Kramer. *Jimi Hendrix Sessions*. London: Little Brown, 1995

Mitchell, Mitch and John Platt. *The Hendrix Experience*. London: Pyramid, 1990

Redding, Noel and Carol Appleby. *Are You Experienced?* London: Fourth Estate, 1990